Mavis the Song Thrush

The Slug and Snail Terminator

First published in August 2016
by
Langford Press, 32 Eastfield,
Narborough, Kings Lynn,
Norfolk PE32 1SS
www.langford-press.co.uk

A CIP Record for this book is
available from the British Library
ISBN 978-1-904078-78-4

Designed by MRM Graphics Ltd
Printed in Spain under the supervision
of MRM Graphics Ltd, Winslow

Mavis the Song Thrush
The Slug and Snail Terminater

by John Miles
and
artwork by Barry Robson

Myweebooks

Langford Press

Mavis the Song Thrush

Mavis starts life in an egg in a mud-lined nest with dry grasses on the outside. Her mother sits for 15 days incubating the eggs so that Mavis can develop in the egg and finally use her 'egg tooth' to break open the egg. Subsequently, she rolls into the nest along with her brothers and sisters. Her mother takes the broken egg away from the nest to prevent predators such as crows and magpies seeing the bright inner egg.
The nest is protected by thick thorns and leaves next to a window ledge

in a house in West Bromwich in the Midlands. This shrub called pyracantha was planted by the owners of the house, the Guptas, to give flowers in the spring and bright coloured berries in the autumn.
Its other name is 'firethorn'. Mr and Mrs Gupta are keen gardeners and love to see wildlife in their small garden. Mr Gupta cuts the pyracantha each year to keep the shrub thick which results in lots of flowers for the bees followed by berries for the birds. This dense foliage keeps the song thrushs' nest away from preying eyes.

West Bromwich is a misspelling of West 'Broom' as the town was built on a habitat called heathland where the shrubby broom, gorse and hawthorn would have been growing wild on the heathland, making a habitat for the song thrush.

The local football team, West Bromwich Albion, even have their ground called the Hawthorns and the song thrush on their badge as their mascot due to their former players enjoying the song of the thrush.
This team is part of the community and always will be.

The Guptas' small garden has several features which attract Mavis's parents to nest here.

Firstly, there is more thick cover consisting of cotoneaster, snowberry, yew, mahonia, holly, rowan and berberis.

Mr Gupta prunes all of these. Each one has berries at a different time of year.

This cover is important when Mavis leaves the nest as predators have an easy job if there are only low flower beds and open lawn.

Mavis needs to keep to the cover to stay alive in the first few weeks of leaving the nest. Gardens are essential for creating a home for nature.

ROBSON '14

Another great attraction is a garden pond. Water snails can be added to the diet of land snails and slugs, part of the diet of the song thrush, helping Mrs Gupta keep her vegetables from being eaten and covered in slime!

Sadly, many gardens are covered with slug pellets which kill the slugs and snails thus preventing the song thrush from a helping of free food.

In addition, the song thrush can be affected by the poisons and die.

Today the combination of a poorly set out garden and the usage of these slug pellets mean that few song thrushes are now found in many of these gardens.

"Slugs and snails are here to break down vegetation which keeps the soil fertile," says Mr Gupta.

The stones around the pond are used as anvils by Mavis's parents to smash the shells of the snails in order to eat the soft parts inside, leaving a pile of shells.

Mavis has to learn this technique from her parents. The anvil played a big part in West Bromwich's industrial past as the forged steel anvil

was used to work metals into shape after being heated by burning coal; the other name for this region is the Black Country.
The local Black Country Industrial Museum still shows a living history of the area.

Due to the protection given by the shrubs in this garden, Mavis and her brothers and sisters soon become independent of their parents and start to move around the neighbourhood.
Their favourite areas are the sports fields across the street and the rough ground with trees and shrubs next door.
Worms are their food on the sports fields while rowan berries are beginning to ripen in the rough ground.

A real bully is their cousin, the mistle thrush, who wants the berries for himself.

Even the new migrant arrivals, the fieldfare and the redwing from Scandinavia, are being pushed around by this bully.

They all have to find a rowan tree that the mistle thrush does not want to protect.

Alternatively, they can wait for his back to be turned then fly in!

Like the new arrivals, song thrushes are migrants and often move away from their place of birth.

Many tend to go a short way in mild winters and are called partial migrants.

Hard winters can see them leave Britain and head into the Mediterranean countries.

Here it may be warmer with plenty of food but they face new dangers such as people shooting and trapping them to eat.

Even special hunting dates are given in some countries, especially for the song thrush.

Mavis is going to try a new area in Cornwall. She will fly at night when the stars shine so that she can navigate using a special compass in her head passed down from generations of song thrushes.
Night time will be quite safe to fly with most predators tucked away asleep.

But pollution of the night sky with electric lights, especially in big cities, has allowed the peregrine falcon to feed in the dead of night.
No one seems to want to put an end to this horrible light pollution! Mavis must fly high out of the glare of lights from the big cities if she is going to stay safe.

As the natural light starts to herald a new day, Mavis is over Cornwall and drops down towards a very green area with an old clay quarry next to it. The clay from this disused quarry has been extracted and transported to the Midlands for the making of pottery. In the quarry there are some funny-looking giant half golf balls surrounded by greenery.
Mavis drops into a tree for cover to rest her tired body.

Her first thoughts are to preen her feathers to keep them suitable for flying and to keep her body warm.
She uses her beak to extract waxy oil from a gland by her tail to spread over the feathers to keep them in shape and waterproof.
Then it is time to have a short sleep before looking for food to build up her energy after the long flight.

Mavis does not know but she has landed in an eco-park. This is the Eden Project which has 1,000s of plants, shrubs and trees from around the world. These domes which are in fact giant greenhouses consist of hundreds of hexagonal and pentagonal inflated plastic cells supported by steel frames.

The first dome simulates a tropical environment and the second a Mediterranean environment; these domes are used to educate the visiting public about the world's flora and its many uses including feeding the human population. Mavis is lucky as the park is full of food which is needed to keep her going through the winter.

As a charity caring for the world, there will be none of those deadly poisonous slug pellets used around here.
What message to the public would that give if thrushes and hedgehogs were suffering en masse?
The project does have to use organic slug pellets though, which do not harm other animals.
These are often based on little creatures called nematodes which are very small worm-type creatures which actually eat the slugs and snails and other pests that feed on the many plants in the Project domes.
This means that Mavis can digest the slugs and snails with nematodes inside them with no adverse effect.

Mavis soon settles down to her new home and finds the Project to her liking. One day she is near one of the big greenhouses and notices the door open. In she goes to explore the surroundings.

She has entered the Mediterranean dome. This is full of plants from that region. She is not alone. Both the robin and the wren find this a great place to live. Robins love feeding on worms and wrens love feeding on spiders.

The winter sun is much hotter in here due to the microclimate.

Sprinklers come on instead of rain to water the plants.

Mavis bathes in a puddle and then flies up to a perch next to the 'glass' to dry off and preen her feathers.

One day she is preening away and does not notice that a male sparrowhawk on the other side has spied her.

The sparrowhawk has not seen the 'glass' and comes diving low across the ground to snatch Mavis for lunch. Bang!

The sparrowhawk hits the 'glass' and falls to the ground. Fortunately, he has hit his chest not his neck and is not dead.

Across Britain many birds lose their lives hitting the clear glass, especially of conservatories and large windows, as the view makes the birds think they can fly on to another part of their territory.

This time Mavis is lucky but will have tokeep her wits about her when returning to the real world outside the Mediterranean dome.

It is soon time to head north again with extra daylight in the dying winter months and find a partner to start a new generation of thrushes. Mavis returns to West Bromwich where she finds her parents back in the garden where she was born. No room here for her so she moves a short way down Forge Lane named after the industrial past using an anvil!

She continues past Forge Mill Farm, a working dairy farm open to the public, and finally into Sandwell Valley. Here is a country park and bird reserve offering her large amounts of scrub to nest in, and plenty of food. There are already a number of male song thrushes singing in an attempt to attract a mate.

One in particular catches her interest. He is singing the commonly repeated song with a number of extras thrown in. This male can emulate a car alarm from the nearby car park and even the ringing of a mobile phone. Song is not the only thing Mavis should be looking at. The size of the male's territory will give evidence of the amount of food available to bring up the kids. And, to make sure the nest is safe from predators, a good thick shrub with plenty of thorns is needed to keep them out. Mavis flies into the territory of this male and has a good look around. This looks perfect. Now she needs to attract the attention of the male and get ready for her first breeding season, hopefully as a successful mum!

Present books in the same series:

Kitty the Toon, Screamer the Swift,
Gowk the Cuckoo, Horace the Peregrine and Fred the Chaffinch

Forthcoming Titles:

Belle the Barn Owl and Henry the Hen Harrier